RISE UP

Lisa Evans

RISE UP

OBERON BOOKS
LONDON

WWW.OBERONBOOKS.COM

First published in 2015 by Oberon Books Ltd
521 Caledonian Road, London N7 9RH
Tel: +44 (0) 20 7607 3637 / Fax: +44 (0) 20 7607 3629
e-mail: info@oberonbooks.com
www.oberonbooks.com

A catalogue record for this book is available from the British
Library.

PB ISBN: 9781783199938
E ISBN: 9781783199945

Cover design by Robbie Lockie at La Veritá / Theatre Centre

Visit www.oberonbooks.com to read more about all our books
and to buy them. You will also find features, author interviews and
news of any author events, and you can sign up for e-newsletters
so that you're always first to hear about our new releases.

Characters

DAYZ
Black, female performer.

EM
Black, female performer.

TY
Black, male performer.

CJ
White, male performer.

Form
Fluid storytelling in which actors can move from character
to character with precise and efficient movement.
The piece should be played with truth but not naturalistically.

SCENE 1

Only EM, TY and DAYZ are on stage in an awkward pre-set waiting to start the show. TY looks at his watch. EM shrugs. They start without CJ.

BRITISH ACTORS' SPOKEN WORD: ENSEMBLE
> It's quite okay to be scared.
> It's all right to feel fright.
> Only fools aren't afraid
> When they challenge the might
> Of how it is now and has always been done,
> So what if it's wrong and that some
> One, somewhere is underfoot.
> It's how you move the air before you.
> There are forces out there

CJ enters, shades on, earphones in, happily unaware he's late. Suddenly gets it, shocked the others carry on valiantly while he acts being 'very quiet' and mouthing 'sorry', thereby drawing attention to himself.

> Want no good to bear
> From the hopes and the dreams of a better world,
> Who don't see the beauty of all that's around you, beyond you,
> Framed in the windows of a greyhound bus.

TY: Stop. Stop.

TY glares at CJ. EM is exaggeratedly patient.

CJ: You started without me.

EM: Because you was late.

CJ: I forgot the time.

EM: That doesn't make it any earlier.

CJ: Wasn't my fault. It was er…

He looks to the audience for support, for an excuse. He comes up with one and then enjoys embellishing it.

The bus. Yeah, and the train, the coach, the plane. *(To audience.)* Gridlock. Yeah.

Yeah they were late, full, couldn't get on, couldn't get off, got stuck in the door, lost my ticket, lost my pass. Nightmare.

EM: He forgot to go to the toilet.

CJ grins, she's right. DAYZ brings on his white bow.

TY: Again.

CJ: Sorree.

(To audience.) Man got to look his best. Know what I mean? And on the subject, I'm not wearing no bow in my hair.

He drops the bow on the floor. DAYZ picks it up.

EM: Act like a doormat, girl, that's how they'll treat you.

DAYZ: Sorry. Sorry.

TY: Can we get on, please?

CJ: I'm not wearing no little old lady hats neither. I got an image, you know what I'm saying?

EM: It is 1961, United States of America, where all men are created equal.

CJ: Except in the Southern States which have their own rules – called Jim Crow – about who can go where.

EM: People have been protesting against segregation in movie theatres, schools, and restaurants but things aren't moving fast enough, especially on the interstate buses travelling through the deep South where white people

(She indicates CJ.)

sit up front.

CJ: I told you, no more old lady hats.

TY: You're an actor.

CJ: So, I'll act being a white lady. It'll be cool.

TY: *(Worried.)* He'll screw it up.

EM: *(To audience.)* White people, like this little old lady *(CJ.)* sit up the front of the buses. And black people *(TY.)* sit at the back.

TY: In the bus stations, there's clean white toilets and white restaurants out the front, and out back there's crummy black toilets, and sometimes, for blacks only, the kinda restaurant even the roaches ignore.

CJ: And you do not go in the wrong one – oh man, you don't.

DAYZ: Until now – when the Congress of Racial Equality asks for volunteers to become Freedom Riders who will set out to change the world by simply boarding a bus.

ALL: And Jim Crow said

CJ: Who?

TY: You know. *Beat.* You do know.

CJ: *(Lying.)* I do. But tell me again anyway?

TY: White folks in the south who believe in the Jim Crow rules. And the Klan, man. White supremacist Southern dudes like dressing up in long white robes, little pointy hats. And burning crosses.

CJ: *(Remembering.)* Hate blacks, Jews, immigrants, well most people except themselves. I remember now.

TY: Good.

ALL: And Jim Crow said.

ENSEMBLE SPOKEN WORD

JIM CROW/TY: You getting on the bus?
    You know where you supposed to sit?

EM: And the Riders said.

    RIDERS talk to the audience.

RIDER/CJ: You brave enough to get on the bus?

JIM CROW/TY: You know the rules?

JIM CROW/DAYZ: Ain't the same for everyone, no sir.

RIDER/CJ: Y'all getting on the bus be prepared for trouble.

RIDER/EM: They taking bad behaviour to a whole new level.

JIM CROW/TY: You sit where you allowed or you git.
    This ain't a matter of choice, oh no, so,
    This the way it's done this side of the line.

JIM CROW/DAYZ: Don't come sniffing round my place cos
    What's mine is mine
    and has always been and that's fine
    by me and my kind.

RIDER/CJ: We don't ask for no trouble we just come to say
Our dollar's the same and when we pay
for a ticket to ride all the way
from DC down to New Orleans,

RIDER/EM: Need a pee or a cuppa tea or a place to be,

RIDER/CJ: We want the same facilities, civilities, utilities
As the next man or woman who pay their buck
For a seat on the bus and don't give a
Damn for your signs that say

RIDER/EM: No coloureds welcome here this day.

JIM CROW/TY: Don't you come down tell me how to live my life.

JIM CROW/DAYZ: This God's own country,

JIM CROW/TY: Me, my wife
Got a way of doing things suits us great.

JIM CROW/DAYZ: Don't tolerate agitators in the Southern States.

JIM CROW/TY: You don't like our ways you turn around,
Go
Take your skinny ass
Back up north,

JIM CROW/DAYZ: Forth with.

RIDER/CJ: We don't want no trouble.

JIM CROW/DAYZ: So stay at home, mind your own damn business.

JIM CROW/TY: Leave us alone to do things the way
They always been done this side of the line
Where it's fine
To have one rule for one
And one for another.

RIDER/CJ: We don't want no trouble.

RIDER/EM: We here as brothers and sisters asking for justice.

RIDER/CJ: Asking for change.

JIM CROW/TY: We don't tolerate trouble

JIM CROW/DAYZ: Trouble

JIM CROW/TY: Trouble.
We don't tolerate.

JIM CROW/DAYZ: No we don't, won't.

JIM CROWS TOGETHER: We won't have it.

RIDER/CJ: You getting on the bus?

RIDER/EM: You sure you brave enough to get on the bus?

TY assigns roles.

TY: Hank *(CJ.)* is a young black student in the Southern States of America, first of his family to go to college, which makes Hank's mother *(EM.)* and father *(TY.)* extremely proud.

DAYZ: Erm, excuse me?

TY: And of course, there's Hank's little sister, Lucille.

SCENE 2

MOTHER: What do you think? Ain't I going to be the proudest, best dressed mama on that entire university campus? We won't let you down, oh no.

HANK: It doesn't matter, Mom.

MOTHER: First in our family to get a university education, you think we're going to turn up to your graduation in old clothes? We been putting money aside for the whole three years for that suit of your Pa's. Now you promise me, no more trouble this semester?

HANK: Well, I wanted to talk with you about /

MOTHER: No. Absolutely no. No such thing is happening here. Your protesting season is done, boy.

HANK: The time is come, Mom. We have a constitution says all men are equal. Except here in the south they don't seem to know that. We have rights.

MOTHER: Rights to have your head caved in.

FATHER: And he the one with the brains in the family.

LUCILLE: Hello?

FATHER: Lucille, this is not about you. Not today.

MOTHER: I sent you to Nashville to study, not to aggravate white folks. What's it matter who sit where? You all looking up at the same screen anyways.

HANK: This time it's not about protesting the movie theatres, Mom.

MOTHER: No?

HANK: I want to be a Freedom Rider.

FATHER: A what?

MOTHER: No.

FATHER: What he talking about now?

MOTHER: I don't know but it sound dangerous. So, no.

HANK: Please, just listen. I been chosen to be one of the Riders on the interstate buses travelling from Washington DC down to New Orleans.

FATHER: You want to go on a bus ride, hundreds of miles cross America, when you got your final exams to sit?

HANK: It's not a vacation. It's to challenge the segregation in the rest rooms and restaurants in the southern states.

MOTHER: Don't let him do it.

HANK: Things got to change. If we don't make it happen, who will? Please Pa?

FATHER: Boy, this like you asking me to sign your death warrant.

HANK: Please? I gotta go now.

FATHER: I said no.

EM: Lucille drives Hank to catch the bus.

CJ makes car noises.

TY: We're not doing noises.

CJ: But it'd be good. If we did. There's a lot of buses /

TY: No

CJ: Like we could have cop cars /

TY: No

CJ: Ambulances?

TY: No.

CJ: Teeny tiny train?

DAYZ/TY/EM: No!

CJ: Just asking.

TY: Just telling.

CJ: Ooooh.

EM: Lucille drives Hank to catch the bus.

LUCILLE stands beside HANK as the driver.

HANK: Sure do appreciate the ride, Sis.

LUCILLE: Keep my foot down we'll catch up by the next stop. Only you could miss the bus to DC to catch the Freedom Bus.

HANK: I never been to DC.

LUCILLE: Me neither. I wish I was coming too.

HANK: You'll give mom my letter?

LUCILLE: Yup.

HANK: Will you tell her you gave me a ride?

LUCILLE: I ain't that stupid.

HANK: Thanks.

LUCILLE: Don't get hurt.

HANK: I'm fine.

LUCILLE: I know you fine now, you doing what you want to. But me, I won't be allowed outa the house ever again if anything happen to you. You know that. Do not forget it.

HANK: Bye Sis.

DAYZ: Lucille looked heartbroken to be left behind, as Hank stared out of the back window of the Greyhound bus – he wasn't allowed to sit at the front.

SCENE 3

TY: Tired and nervous after his journey, Hank arrives at the Quaker Centre in Washington DC, where the other Freedom Riders are all assembled for the first time.

THORA/EM: Come in, come in. Welcome to Washington. You must be…?

HANK: Hank, Ma'am.

THORA: Oh those lovely Southern manners. The name's Thora. And don't let being the youngest person here intimidate you. Some of us aren't as old as we look.

HANK: How many Freedom Riders are there?

THORA: Thirteen, black and white together. We got all sorts, a professor – that's my husband, the old white guy with the beard over there – a couple of journalists. Those two black dudes are a folksinger – he's good, from New York and – collar's a giveaway – a reverend. We got teachers /

HANK: And a student.

THORA: Of course. Your parents must be upset you're missing graduation.

HANK: No.

THORA: No?

HANK: Well, yeah but…

THORA: How come?

Beat.

Hank?

HANK: They don't know yet. My sister Lucille telling them later.

THORA: What about your professors?

HANK: Nope. Them neither.

THORA: Holy /

HANK: Yeah. Right.

THORA: Myrna, hey Myrna honey, weren't you still in school, first time you took action?

MYRNA/DAYZ: Oh yeah. Greensboro, North Carolina was the first time we protested a whites-only restaurant. White man threatened to tar and feather us.

Second place we ask to be served the manager ordered the old black guy mopping the floor to chuck his dirty water over us.

HANK: One evening when we were protesting in Fairfield, the white manager leaves, locks the doors and turns on the roach killer. It was like a gas chamber.

THORA: How d'you get out?

HANK: Broke the glass.

THORA: And it makes you mad, right?

HANK: Fit to bust.

MYRNA: Amen to that.

JIM/TY: Listen up everyone. Those who don't know me, my name is Jim. And the reason I, a white man, am part of the Freedom Ride is because, whereas I can walk away from this struggle, my black brothers and sisters cannot. They do not have that choice. So we need to stand together and stand firm for the good of all Americans. Now, you've all been chosen, black and white, to participate in the Freedom Ride because of your commitment to peaceful resistance. We need to get in training so you can handle what will surely come at you – the name calling, the abuse, the intimidation.

CJ: What? Like what?

TY: You can't have forgotten already?

CJ: I got a lot to remember.

TY: *(Sighing.)* Okay. Go for it.

EM: *(Aggressive.)* What gave you the right to have an opinion?

CJ: I just asked /

DAYZ: You were told to shut up. So shut up you liar, you total wasteman.

TY: Hands above your head. Up against the car.

DAYZ: Hands out your pockets. Stand where I can see you.

TY: You're not with your crew now, pull your trousers up.

EM: Your sort not wanted round here.

DAYZ: You're just trouble.

CJ: But I /

ALL: Shut up, shut your mouth, shut up!

CJ: *(Shaken.)* That's harsh man. Stop it. Stop it.

TY: *(Reasonable.)* That's how they did it.

EM: Taste of what was to come.

DAYZ: Preparation.

TY: So. Training for Passive Resistance. Been used all over the world. Remember now?

CJ: Yes. Yes. Face of keen boy remembering it.

TY: *(To audience.)* Most important thing is the Freedom Riders don't react, no matter what the provocation. They're going into the deep South to challenge segregation, not to get into fights.

CJ: *(Playing to the audience.)* I don't do fighting. I got to take care of the face, right?

TY: Just do Hank.

HANK: You going to be okay with this, Ma'am?

THORA: Just cos I'm old and got skin like a plucked chicken don't mean I haven't seen my share of protest. I believe my students know me as a tough old bird.

HANK: You're not afraid?

THORA: There is a possibility that we won't be served. There is a possibility we will be arrested. There's a possibility we will be hurt.

JIM: Who's made a will?

All hands go up except for HANK.

HANK: *(Starts to laugh then sees they're serious.)* All I got in the world's in my bag. I got nothing to leave.

JIM: We'll be travelling on two scheduled interstate buses, one Trailways, one Greyhound, with regular passengers on board. Riders should mingle with them, talk to them and represent the cause of social justice openly and honestly.

MYRNA: On each bus, one black Rider will sit in a seat normally reserved for whites. At least one interracial pair will sit in adjoining seats and the remaining Riders will be scattered throughout the bus, with one Rider on each bus taking the role of designated observer.

JIM: This Rider will obey the conventions of segregated travel so that at least one Rider will avoid arrest and be able to contact the CORE offices or arrange legal counsel for those who are arrested.

MYRNA: There will be no police escort and no national press coverage. Once we leave DC and head into the Deep South, we'll be on our own.

JIM: Listen up, it's time! On the bus!

DAYZ: Ahead stretched 13 days and 1500 miles of deep southern highway.

SCENE 4

BRITISH ACTOR SPOKEN WORD:

TY: It's quite okay to be scared.
    It's all right to feel fright.
    Only fools aren't afraid
    When they challenge the might
    Of how it is now and has always been done.

Who cares if it's wrong and that some
One, somewhere is underfoot?
There are forces out there
Want no good to bear
From the hopes and the dreams of a better world.
Who don't see the beauty of all that's around you, beyond you
Framed in the windows of a Greyhound bus.
Caught between curtains, sun whitening, eye brightening,
The shimmering haze across cornfields,
The cool under live oak and sassafras trees.
It's how you move the air before you.
First part is the easy part,
The start
of something bigger than you,
Few.
America's a beautiful country.
It's the land of opportunity
Not community, no colour immunity.
The shade, the grade, of the black on your back counts for
something.
They call it home of the brave.
They say it's the land of the free.
Right now on the road you thinking,
This ain't gonna be
Bad as we
Feared.
Black and white together going to make a stand,
Bring overdue change across this new found land,
And it's going to be all right, right?
And it's okay to be scared.

Under the following speech the other three say the places the buses
travel through, moving south. 'Farmville, Lynchburg, Danville,
Greensboro, Charlotte, Rock Hill, Winsboro, Colombia, Sumter,
Augusta, Athens, Atlanta'.

EM: Their entire world is framed by the windows of the interstate buses and the towns and terminals they step into. And so far it seems to be going well.

TY: Next stop, Anniston, Alabama.

SCENE 5

DAYZ: As they approach Anniston it's such a beautiful day their hearts lift. It is quiet and sunny, the sky is blue, the scenery through the bus window is breath-taking.

EM: *(Handing out role.)* There is a little white girl playing out front of her parents' grocery store.

CJ: No bows.

EM: Little white girl

(CJ adjusts to the role.)

With a little white southern voice.

WHITE GIRL/CJ: Okey dokey.

I am 12 years old. My folks have the grocery store beside the house and the name of it is Forsyth and Son Grocery. No black people ever get served in our store. My Moma says...

MA/TY: We keep things nice. Our customers like things a certain way.

EM and DAYZ become white lady shoppers who always speak in unison like a couple of budgies.

SHOPPERS: Oh we do. We do.

MA: And we don't want no trouble.

SHOPPERS: No trouble.

22

MA: The coloured folks can do they shopping down their part of town.

WHITE GIRL: Why?

MA: You understand, they eat different things.

SHOPPERS: Mmm. Things.

WHITE GIRL: Like what, Moma?

MA: Just different, honey, that's all you need to know. Take my word for it, if folk looks different, they gonna eat different, they gonna be different.

SHOPPERS: Different, different, different.

MA: Can't change that. How the good Lord made us.
And I don't want you go catching nothing.

SHOPPERS: *(Shuddering.)* Bad habits.

WHITE GIRL: Like what, Moma?

MA: Like asking questions all the time. We like things they way they are. Everybody know their place. And we all happy that way.

SHOPPERS: We happy.

WHITE GIRL: Everybody happy!

Till one day *(Nominating TY.)* Big Uncle George says

UNCLE GEORGE/TY: We hear there are some agitators coming down from the North. But don't you worry, darlin', me and some of my friends got a surprise party planned for them.

WHITE GIRL: And he kind of laughs. And I do too cos I love a party.

EM: On the bus.

DAYZ: The Freedom Riders don't have any sense of fear as they drive into Anniston, despite warnings about the white mob, who are gathering in large numbers outside the bus terminal.

(DAYZ indicates TY as MOB.)

MOB/TY: Hey, stop. Stop them. This bus full of Yankees, Jews and uppity blacks sitting in the wrong place. We'll show them their place.

(Shouting at the occupants of the bus.)

Hey! You, you in the bus. You in our country now.
No darkies and Yankees going to tell us how to behave.

DAYZ: They're surrounded by trucks and cars full of white folks, some still dressed in their Sunday come-from-church clothes, banging on the side of the bus, shouting hate.

EM: Then finally the driver eases them out and they get hopeful, driving out of town.

MOB/TY: You take your filthy ways back up North or we going to string you up.

RIDER/DAYZ: Thank god we outa that place.

RIDER/EM: They following us – can't we drive faster?

MOB/TY: Stop them. Stop them negro lovers.

RIDER/DAYZ: What's that noise?

RIDER/EM: Sweet Jesus, the tyres. The tyres are flat.

MOB/TY: We got 'em now, boys.

WHITE GIRL: There is a commotion outside so I walk to the front of the store to see what is going on. The bus is swerving about all over the road. It slows. Stops. The driver gets out, looks at the tyres and when he sees how flat and hopeless they are, he just walks away.

RIDER/DAYZ: You can't leave us here!

WHITE GIRL: He just walks away as the crowd surrounds the bus.

UNCLE GEORGE/TY: Let's have us some fun.

RIDER/DAYZ: We're surrounded.

RIDER/EM: Our Father which art in heaven, hallowed be thy name.

UNCLE GEORGE: You going to roast in the fires of hell.

RIDER/DAYZ: Stand back!

WHITE GIRL: I watch as a man raises his arm out of the crowd.

RIDER/EM: Thy kingdom come, thy will be done,

RIDER/DAYZ: Stand back from the window!

MOB/TY: You there, give us a hand.

RIDER/EM: On earth as it is in heaven.

UNCLE GEORGE: We'll show you a real southern welcome.

WHITE GIRL: And with a crowbar he's breaking out one of the back windows of the bus.

RIDER/EM: Give us this day our daily bread.

UNCLE GEORGE: Burn negro lovers, burn.

RIDER/DAYZ: They got torches.

RIDER/EM: Forgive us our trespasses,

RIDER/DAYZ: They going to burn us? Alive?

UNCLE GEORGE/TY: Throw it in!

RIDER/EM: As we forgive them that trespass against us.

WHITE GIRL: There's a flash of flame and smoke all billowing black.

RIDER/DAYZ: Can't see.

RIDER/EM: Can't breathe.

UNCLE GEORGE: Burn them! Burn them alive!

RIDER/EM: Get the door open.

RIDER/DAYZ: I'm trying.

RIDER/EM: Try harder. Two, three, together and push!

UNCLE GEORGE: Don't let 'em out.

WHITE GIRL: There's coughing and screaming and banging against the door. And the reason they can't get out is the men leaning on the outside of the door.

RIDER/EM: Deliver us from evil.

RIDER/DAYZ: We all going to die.

UNCLE GEORGE: Oh my god, the engine's on fire. Move back. The fuel tank's gonna blow.

WHITE GIRL: Boom! The bus door bursts open and people spilling out onto the ground.

UNCLE GEORGE: Don't let them get away.

WHITE GIRL: All around people are gagging, crawling, trying to cough the smoke out of their chests.

RIDER/DAYZ: Water. Please give me water.

UNCLE GEORGE: Go inside now.

WHITE GIRL: Neighbours throwing stones at the people on the ground, hitting them with iron pipes.

RIDER/DAYZ: Oh god, I need water.

UNCLE GEORGE: This not your business. Go inside.

TY joins the other RIDERS under the next speech, coughing, calling for help and water.

WHITE GIRL: But I don't go. Instead I am walking right out into the middle of that crowd. I pick me out one person. I wash her face. I hold her. I give her water to drink. Here lady, drink this water. It's good and cold. Make you feel better. She real thirsty. As soon as I think she going to be okay, I pick out somebody else. And then somebody else. It was the right thing to do.

PATROLMAN/EM: Okay, this the highway patrol, you've had your fun. Let's move back.

WHITE GIRL: I never forget this day in all my life. 'Fore this, my folks always right, telling me mind my business. Not any more. This is my business. No matter I am from the Jim Crow South, I have a choice.

EM: The people on the Trailways bus don't know that the Greyhound bus has been burned in Anniston and the Riders are sitting on the ground covered in blood. They're going into Birmingham, a city run by Police Chief Bull Connor.

TY takes his stance. EM has fun at his expense.

So called because he looked like a bulldog

TY gives her a look. Don't think I can do it eh? and transforms.

BULL/TY: *(On phone.)* Yes. Who is this?

KLAN/CJ: A member, a senior member, of the Klan. That's all I'm prepared to say.

BULL: And?

KLAN: This is a Fiery Cross summons to all Klan members in all surrounding states. Be sure and be at the Birmingham bus terminal tomorrow cos you're going to see action.

BULL: How many coming?

KLAN: Thousand or so.

BULL: Fine. You do know you phoned the police station?

KLAN: Shoot.

BULL: Yeah. Bull Connor here, Chief of Police.

KLAN: I musta misdialled.

BULL: As it happens you saved me a call. Listen up. Tomorrow when that bus arrives, I will give you people fifteen minutes to burn, maim, bomb those negro lovers, I don't give a goddam.

KLAN: What about your police officers?

BULL: Seeing as how it's Mother's Day, I'm giving them time off to spend with their Moms.

KLAN: Gee Bull, you're all heart.

BULL: I sure am and I will guarantee your people that not one soul will be arrested in that fifteen minutes.

KLAN: Only doing God's work.

BULL: Exactly. Protecting our way of life. Good day, Hubert.

KLAN: Good da... How did you know it was me?

BULL: I run Birmingham. I know everything. We don't call it the Magic City for nothing.

SCENE 7

DAYZ: Birmingham, Alabama. 15 minutes. What can you do in 15 minutes?

REPORTER/EM: Care to comment, Governor Patterson?

PATTERSON/CJ: *(Reasonable and charming.)* See this. We are white Americans who live in the South. The more they try to force us unto changing something, the worse the reactions will be.

BRITISH ACTOR'S SPOKEN WORD: SOLO:
It's Mothers' day and the weather is fine
As the bus draws into downtown Birmingham.
Man, it's quiet,
Like the city has stopped
Dead
In its tracks.

Smacks
Of no god or good,
This sunny Sunday celebrating motherhood.
Not a child in sight
On the street.
The feet
Are behind closed doors, windows shuttered.
Muttered
Slogans growing louder as they
Turn into the bus station.
Anticipation of conflagration.
Remember, non-violent demonstration.
Hearts bumping, breathing shallow.
Rehearse the drill
They will follow
Today, tomorrow,
Till the signs come down
From Whites Only cafes in this part of town.
If there's an attack
Do not fight back.
Against chains and spikes and tire irons
Baseball bats and hammers and wrenches?
They want to kill them.
They want them dead.
53 stitches in one white head,
For being a traitor, for being a mensch.
While outside, on a bench,
The cops watch the hands on their watches
For fifteen blood flowing, skin tearing, bone shearing
minutes.
And it's over.
But it's not.
They got
To go on.
Or what does it say about the laws of the land,

If might beats right, and nine men and women,
Black and white
Might,
Quite likely,
Never get over what happened to them
On Mothers' Day in Birmingham?
They resolve to go on till the song they are singing
Drowns out the ringing
Of blows to the head,
Or they are dead.

SCENE 8

CJ: Hidden in safe houses in Birmingham, the Riders decide to go on. Only trouble is, even if they are prepared to face the mob again, no bus driver can be found willing to drive them. They're trapped.

THORA: So. It's over.

MYRNA: The Freedom Rides are over.

JIM: Shall we take a vote? All those in favour of going home?

MYRNA: While we're still alive.

THORA: Carried unanimously.

MYRNA: Just one thing. If no one will drive us, how do we get out of this place?

SCENE 9

Sound cue of the Stars and Stripes. They put their hands on their chests in gesture of allegiance.

CJ: Meanwhile, the President of the United States of America, John F Kennedy,

(He indicates EM.)

Who is tall,

(EM stretches herself up.)

And very charismatic,

(EM smiles.)

Is addressing Congress.

JFK/EM: I believe that this nation should commit itself to achieving the goal, before this decade is out, of landing a man on the moon.

These are extraordinary times. And we face an extraordinary challenge. Our strength as well as our convictions have imposed upon this nation the role of leader in freedom's cause. No role in history could be more difficult or more important. We stand for freedom.

CJ: President Kennedy calls his brother Bobby

CJ indicates himself.

to an early morning meeting at the White House.

JFK/EM: You two know each other, of course. *(To BOBBY.)* As my Aide, John here will be your point of contact while I'm at the summit.

BOBBY shakes hands with the AIDE/TY.

AIDE/TY: Good morning Mr Attorney General sir.

BOBBY K/CJ: Call me Bobby.

AIDE: Yes sir.

JFK: *(Switching off the smile.)* Why isn't Governor Patterson returning my calls?

AIDE: I don't know, Mr President.

JFK: Well what do his office say when you tell them it's President John F Kennedy on the telephone?

AIDE: They say, he's gone fishing, Mr President.

JKF: They're beating those damn Freedom Riders senseless in Birmingham on the national news, and the Governor of Alabama goes fishing?

AIDE: That's the message he's giving.

JFK: Bobby, you got to do something. Get them off those buses. I got meetings with Khrushchev in Vienna in two weeks' time, talking about democracy, for God's sake.

BOBBY: I know. I know.

JFK: After the fiasco with Cuba, the whole damn world is watching us. This 'provocation' here at this time is embarrassing to the Presidency, it is embarrassing to the United States of America.

BOBBY K: We'll calm things down, Mr President, don't worry.

JKF: Send a plane in, get them out of there, whatever it takes, get them back up north and off the front page.

BOBBY K: ⎫
⎬ Yes Sir.
AIDE: ⎭

DAYZ: Back home, beaten, demoralized, the Freedom Riders say goodbye, their dreams over.

SCENE 10

THORA: Myrna, we'll talk soon, yeah? Meet up.

MYRNA: Decide what to do next.

THORA: You know, I used to think all human beings were good at heart. I don't know I believe that any more.

HANK: I hear your husband came round at last, Ma'am?

THORA: He spoke. First time since the coma.

HANK: What'd he say?

THORA: He mostly swore. Profoundly.

HANK: That's good news. Isn't it?

THORA: I guess. Doctors say he won't walk again.

HANK: Jeez. So, all that, for what? What have we achieved?

MYRNA: Folks starting to pay attention.

THORA: One hell of a cost.

MYRNA: We tried our best, Thora. That's all we can do.

THORA: Phone.

HANK: The Freedom Rides are over. I can't believe it.

THORA: Could somebody who's not broken anything get that?

HANK: The Freedom Rides are over.

THORA: Hank! Would you stop saying that!

JIM: *(On phone.)* Hello. Speaking. Yes.

HANK: Over.

JIM: *(On phone.)* Who?

HANK: It's the truth.

MYRNA: What's up? Bad news?

JIM: There's another wave of Freedom Riders heading on down to Birmingham to continue the rides.

THORA: What?

JIM: Yeah. Diane Nash and a group of students.

SCENE 11

BOBBY KENNEDY/CJ: Who the hell is Diane Nash? I thought the Freedom Rides were all over and done with.

AIDE/TY: Well, Mr Attorney General sir, according to the FBI she's a student activist at Fiske University in Nashville.

DIANE/DAYZ: Fellow students. I have been to jail already for protesting against segregation. I know I will go to jail again. I do not shrink from it. You elected me as your leader and as such I say to you, I believe there is a source of power in each of us that we don't realise until we take responsibility. We are the students who have protested and not been broken. We are fresh troops. If we allow the Freedom Ride to stop now, the message will be sent that all you have to do to stop a non-violent campaign is inflict massive violence. Take a break. Go out and think about it for 10 minutes. It'll mean dropping out of school, just as finals come. It's up to you.

BOBBY K: Call her and let her know what's waiting for them.

AIDE: *(On phone.)* Yes, Miss Nash. I understand there are more Freedom Riders coming down from Nashville. Word has it they will be met in Birmingham with extreme violence. You must stop them if you can.

DIANE: They're not going to turn back.

AIDE: You do know I am the official representative of the US Government, speaking from the Attorney General's office?

DIANE: Yes, I do. They're on their way to Birmingham now. They'll be there shortly.

AIDE: Are you listening to me?

DIANE: Yes, sir, I am.

AIDE: Do you not know or care anything about these young people?

DIANE: They are some of my closest friends and they are going to Birmingham.

AIDE: Young woman, do you not understand you're going to get somebody killed?

DIANE: Sir, we made our wills. We know someone will be killed.

AIDE: Then child, for the love of God make it stop.

BRITISH ACTOR'S SPOKEN WORD: SOLO:
    The students knew what they were doing.
    They knew what could happen.
    They talked about it into the night.
    Fright
    Was not an option.
    Not a choice.
    Somebody's voice

Had to be raised.
Or what was the point of the education,
The classes fought and paid for
By parental dedication
And hours of saving,
Craving
A better life for the next generation?
If bigotry's voice is louder than law,
They saw
That nothing had changed since the plantation
And slavery still
Will
Prevail.
The students knew what they were doing.
They knew what could happen.
They talked about it into the night.
Told tales of their folks back in time,
The ancestral line
Of courage
It takes to walk into the tiger's mouth.
The fear of the south.
They talked of beatings and maiming,
Hospitals and pain,
Of how to stand together
To achieve a common aim.
Of hope they'd stand this test
With the best
Of those who came
Before,
Sure,
Though their hearts shook,
They could hear,
Clear
Across the cotton fields,
The bones of their elders

Lying in the graveyards
Rattle
Like a drum beat
Going into battle.
A tune of this is your turn,
This is your time.
Climb
Aboard.
They knew what they were doing.
They knew what could happen.
They talked about it into the night
And chose
To go.

TY: The students arrive in Birmingham and before anything
can happen at the bus station, they are arrested.

SCENE 12

EM: It's cave dark night in the back of the police cars driving
them out of Birmingham. They're being driven by that
bogie man, Chief of police, Bull Connor himself.

RICKY/CJ: Where you taking us?

BULL/TY: Out of harm's way, boy.

RICKY: We have a right to know where we going, sir.

BULL: You in God's own country now, boy. My rules apply.

BERNICE/DAYZ: One of the policeman at the jail said we were
being taken back to Nashville.

BULL: Best you go back where you came from.

FRANCES/EM: Are we still under arrest?

BULL: I let you out of jail, didn't I?

FRANCES: Then can we make a call? Let our folks know we're all right?

BULL: Should have thought of that before you left your university, come on down here telling us how to live. That's what comes of education – nothing but trouble.

FRANCES: We just want to use the same facilities at the bus station.

BERNICE: We're not out to make trouble.

BULL: You lucky I arrested you the minute you set foot on Alabama soil. The good ole Klan boys dying to get their hands on you. You damn lucky to be alive.

RICKY: Why're we stopping?

FRANCES: *(Turning round.)* The other cars are stopping too.

BULL: End of the road folks. Out you get.

RICKY: What's going on? Where is this?

BULL: State line. Alabama. Tennessee.

BERNICE: You said we were being taken to Nashville.

BULL: Did I? Well, you just going to have to find yourselves a train to get there, or maybe a bus.

He laughs.

FRANCES: In the middle of the night? In the middle of nowhere?

TY: The police drive away leaving them in pitch darkness.

DAYZ: Black kids. In the middle of Klan territory.

MARVIN/TY: Do you think they're waiting for us?

RICKY: Let's get off the road into the countryside, more chance of finding a black homestead other side of the tracks.

BERNICE: Stick together.

MARVIN: What's that noise?

FRANCES: Just my heart knocking to stay alive.

RICKY: Please God may there not be a lynch mob.

TY: Every twig cracking step they take they wait for a flash of burning torches,

DAYZ: The closing circle of hooded men in white robes,

EM: Fingers itching to string them up and hang them by the neck.

BERNICE: Look. Up ahead.

RICKY: How do we know it's not a white folks house?

BERNICE: No white man going to live this back of beyond.

RICKY: Knock on the door.

MARVIN: No, you knock on the door.

BERNICE: I'll do it.

OLD BLACK MAN/TY: What do you want?

FRANCES: Go on.

RICKY: What?

FRANCES: Tell him.

RICKY: I'm so sorry to trouble you, sir, but we're the Freedom Riders. We need your help.

OLD BLACK MAN: I can't let you in. I'm sorry. I just can't.

RICKY: Please sir. We won't stay long but if you could just let us make one quick call?

OLD BLACK MAN: No. It's dark, it's late. I can't. If you knew how much trouble we'd be in if anyone found out.

BERNICE: If we could please just speak to the lady of the house?

OLD BLACK MAN: Lady?

BERNICE: That's what my Moma always taught me to say.

OLD BLACK MAN: I told them to go way.

OLD BLACK WOMAN/EM: Why? Who is it? What they want?

OLD BLACK MAN: She wants the lady.

OLD BLACK WOMAN/EM: Why, Lord save us, they just chillun. Honey, let them right in. Quick, fore some cracker see you.

The old couple become RIDERS again listening to the phone call.

FRANCES: *(On phone.)* Diane?

DIANE/DAYZ: *(On phone.)* This is Diane Nash.

FRANCES: *(On phone.)* It's me, Frances.

DIANE: *(On phone.)* Thank god. You all safe?

FRANCES: *(On phone.)* For tonight anyways.

DIANE: *(On phone.)* No one got hurt?

FRANCES: *(On phone.)* They arrested us at the bus-station before anything could happen.

DIANE: *(On phone.)* So where are you now?

FRANCES: *(On phone.)* Taking shelter, someplace just across the Tennessee border.

DIANE: *(On phone.)* I'll send someone to get you. There's eleven other packages been shipped to Birmingham already.

FRANCES: *(On phone.)* Packages?

DIANE: *(On phone.)* To take your place? Can't say more than that on this phone. If you know what I mean.

FRANCES: *(On phone.)* Oh, packages! Right.

RICKY: What's she say?

FRANCES: FBI are tapping the line.

MARVIN: FBI?

DIANE: *(On phone.)* Car will be with you by the morning. Where d'you want to go?

FRANCES: Another wave of Freedom Riders are on their way down. Diane says do we want to go home to Nashville or join them back in Birmingham?

Beat.

ALL TOGETHER: Birmingham.

PATTERSON/CJ: *(Reasonable and charming.)* People, ordinary people, of the south say to me, 'Governor Patterson, you cannot change a way of life overnight. These people are provoking us.' And I agree.

AIDE/TY: I go down to Alabama at the request of the Attorney General. I am a white government official.

PATTERSON: As your Governor I can't act as nursemaid to encourage agitators.

AIDE: This time, when the buses roll into the bus station in Birmingham Alabama, it's war on the ground.

PATTERSON: I think when they learn that when they go somewhere to create a riot there's not going to be anyone to stand between them and the other crowd, they'll stay home.

AIDE: A big white guy has a Freedom Rider down on the sidewalk with his foot on his neck while another man is trying to put a steel rod through his ear.

PATTERSON: What southern folks – black and white – want is peace and stability.

AIDE: Police in their uniforms just standing there watching.

PATTERSON: These people are here to breach that peace.

AIDE: I go to help. 'I am a Government official'.

PATTERSON: You can't guarantee the safety of a fool.

AIDE: And before I know it, they whirl me round, hit me with a pipe and kick me under a car.

PATTERSON: And that's what these folks are.

AIDE: They don't care who I am. Far as they're concerned, I'm a traitor.

PATTERSON: Just fools.

SCENE 14

EM: Meanwhile, in his offices in Washington, the Attorney General, Bobby Kennedy, was having a bad day.

BOBBY K/CJ: What in the name of heaven is going on down there in Alabama? Get that Nash woman on the phone.

Both on phone.

DIANE/DAYZ: Diane Nash speaking.

BOBBY K: How did this 'situation' come about without our knowledge?

DIANE: We mailed copies of our letter outlining our plans for the Freedom Ride to the President, to the Attorney General Robert Kennedy /

BOBBY K: We never received any letter.

DIANE: Yet again, for the second time in as many weeks, in Birmingham Alabama, American citizens are being beaten and intimidated half to death while state police stand by and do nothing.

BOBBY K: Must have been lost in the mail.

DIANE: We need help. The students who are not injured are on the buses heading south into Montgomery.

BOBBY K: They'll have a police escort.

SCENE 15

MARVIN/TY's head is being tended to by a black woman – MRS TARVER/EM.

MRS TARVER/EM: Hold still Marvin honey, this going to sting.

MARVIN/TY: Then the police just disappear and Len's
    shouting 'Stand together!' and at the front of the mob
    were white women – with babies in their arms – and these
    women are screaming to kill us, beat us to death,
    to 'Git them ni /'

MRS TARVER/EM: Honey, I heard the words before.
    Been called most everything in my time.

MARVIN: Mrs Tarver, Ma'am. It's real kind of you to take me
    in. But are the others going to be okay?

MRS TARVER: Let us pray so. This is one deep wound.
    How many fingers you see?

MARVIN: I just see their faces, spitting on us, aiming for our
    heads with chains and baseball bats, one of them even had
    a pitchfork.

MRS TARVER: That what they got you with? You oughta get a
    Tetanus shot.

MARVIN: They say someone swung at my head with a Coca-
    Cola crate. I don't remember that part.

MRS TARVER: You should have been taken to the hospital.

MARVIN: No black ambulances. I'll be okay. I'm sorry,
    Mrs Tarver, Ma'am, I bled on your nice white counterpane.

MRS TARVER: Child, grievous wrong has been done today.
    The least of it is to my counterpane. May the Lord forgive
    them their fear and hatred and see justice come, amen.

MARVIN: I don't forgive the men who knocked Will unconscious with an iron bar and then stomped on his chest. I don't forgive the man who lifted Len's head where he lay on the ground and held it between his knees so the children could hit and claw him till the blood ran down his face. I don't. I surely don't.

MRS TARVER: Would you like to call your mom, reassure her you alive and walking?

MARVIN nods, suddenly overcome. MRS TARVER comforts him.

I know, child, I know. Like your friend said, we got to stand together.

SCENE 16

MARTIN LUTHER KING/CJ: I have a dream.

TY: Not yet.

CJ: Why not?

TY: Cos Martin Luther King hasn't said it yet.

CJ: You joking me? MLK he was always there during the civil rights thing.

TY: If you remember, he didn't do his I Have a Dream speech till August 1963.

CJ: Whatever.

TY: No. It matters.

EM: One action inspires another.

CJ: Concentrating inspires me to yawn.

EM: Stop clowning around, trying to be popular. Use your brains.

CJ: I do.

EM: For more than just supporting your hairstyle.

CJ: *(Appreciating her wit.)* Nice one, babe.

She gives him a look.

He grins at her.

I just forget stuff.

EM: You need to pay attention, you aren't going to be pretty for ever.

CJ: *(Flexing.)* I work out, I got muscle.

EM: Yeah, in your head. Get holda some facts, surprise him.

(To DAYZ.)

Come on. Do I have to organise everything round here?

DAYZ: Sorry. But…

EM: What?

DAYZ: It's your line.

EM: Right.

After a tense night in Montgomery, Diane Nash receives a phone call.

SCENE 17

Both DIANE and BOBBY KENNEDY are on the phone.

DIANE/DAYZ: You wanted to speak to me Mr Kennedy.

BOBBY K/CJ: Miss Nash, this has got to stop.

DIANE: I agree. Last night in Montgomery, Alabama, an entire congregation of men, women and children come to hear Dr King and the Freedom Riders, was surrounded by a mob of over three thousand people threatening to burn their church to the ground with them in it.

BOBBY K: Early on the Federal Marshalls were sent from Washington to control the situation.

DIANE: 50 postal workers and custom officials who were so useless they choked themselves with their own tear gas? Sir, they were never going to stop the mob.

BOBBY K: Which is why the National Guard was sent in.

DIANE: Not until midnight! After cars were set alight, rocks thrown through the church windows. Those folks, fellow Americans, believed they were going to die in flames.

BOBBY K: But they didn't. This is a regrettable situation. Everyone just needs to cool down.

DIANE: If we cool down any more, sir, we'll be in the freezer.

BOBBY K: You need to get those students out of Alabama.

DIANE: Governor Patterson has done nothing to protect us so far.

BOBBY K: Governor Patterson will do as the President says.

CJ picks up DAYZ' notebook and starts to read it.

SCENE 18

EM: The Riders are given a police escort out of Montgomery and along the highway south.

DOLORES/DAYZ: *(Waving.)* Wave, Granpa.

CJ is busy reading.

Granpa!

EM steps into role.

Wave.

GRANPA/EM: At what, Dolores?

DOLORES: Freedom Riders, on the bus to Jackson. Come on, they the folks who got trapped in the church, on the radio.

GRANPA: How d'you figure that?

DOLORES: Escort of State troopers, six police vehicles and a helicopter? Less the president taken to travelling by bus down to Mississippi, I'm betting that's the Freedom Riders.

GRANPA: Word is, they never going to make it to New Orleans.

DOLORES: Don't you want them to?

GRANPA: I don't wish anyone harm child, but you don't remember how it used to be. We doing fine without poking no nest of snakes. We got us a good business here. Nice house. Car in the garage. How many of those angry folks going to do business with me now?

DOLORES: I think the Freedom Riders doing it for us.

GRANPA: I didn't ask them to come here.

DOLORES: There was women and kids in that church they were going to set fire to.

GRANPA: Exactly. Folks who just want to work, raise their kids proper, go to church and pray. You think we got us this place out of agitating and making trouble?

DOLORES: I guess not.

GRANPA: It's not the way the world works, Dolores honey, you got to look after your own. No one else but me going to take care of my family. It's better to just let things be.

SCENE 19

CJ: In eighteen hundred and sixty five,

Slavery is abolished in the USA.

TY: What the hell…?

CJ: Don't stop me now, I'm on a roll.

He has to keep going or he'll forget it.

90 years later young Emmett Till
Is killed
For whistling at a white woman,
So they say,
In Mississippi, southern USA.
This side of the line segregation doing fine,
In restaurants and rest rooms, schools, stores, buses.

EM: Don't forget Rosa Parks.

CJ: December 55 and the Montgomery Bus Boycott got
Started by
One black woman who refused to stand up.
She was tired from work going home on the bus.
She was tired of giving way, of making no fuss.
She don't cuss,

Just
Refuse
To move.
1957 and nine black kids
Desegregate a high school in Little Rock.
Takes troops and press and national guard.
It's hard
To get to school in Little Rock
If you're black,
Back
In the day.
3 years on in North Carolina,
Black students begin,
To sit in,
Sit down and refuse
To move
Till facilities are the same for all
Who study there,
Whose brains are pink,
Who think
For themselves, not in black or white,
Who think in colour about what's right.
May 61 and CORE decides
To challenge interstate travel with the Freedom Rides.
63, back in Birmingham
Is the Children's Crusade in Alabam
Assaulting kids with dogs and hosing them down
To the ground,
Locking them in jail downtown.
Thousands of kids washed off the street,
Small feet
Marching for justice.
August, all races march on Washington DC.
And Martin Luther King he
Tells the world of his dream

That injustice anywhere is a threat to justice everywhere,
That what affects one directly, affects another indirectly.
His dream, his dream, we all could share.
In Selma 1965 comes Bloody Sunday where
Civil rights marchers are beaten by police.
Three years later, 1968,
The dream is shot.
And Martin Luther King's brave soul flies free
From a balcony of the Lorraine Motel,
Memphis, Tennessee.
And the whole world is watching.

CJ: Wow. Now I get it! This stuff happening makes the next stuff happen.

EM: Well?

TY: Okay. Good.

Beat.

CJ: Cool.

DAYZ: *(Just to CJ.)* You used my notes.

CJ: *(Unrepentant.)* Yeah, they were ace. Thanks Babe.

EM: Don't forget the women. Rosa Parks /

DAYZ: Claudette Colvin was arrested for refusing to get out of her bus seat for a white woman, 9 months before Rosa Parks. And she was only 15.

EM: That a fact?

DAYZ: *(Not confident at first but then with assurance.)* Yes. Yes, it is.

EM: Go girl.

TY: Meanwhile. The Freedom Riders arrive in Jackson, Mississippi,

CJ: and for peacefully protesting the segregated facilities in the bus station, they are arrested, convicted and sent to

SCENE 20

CHORUS:

GUARD/TY: Parchman Penitentiary. Destination Doom.

RIDER/EM: Exercising my constitutional right.

GUARD: Not here in Jackson.

RIDER/DAYZ: Stripped.

RIDER/CJ: Body searched.

RIDER/DAYZ: Humiliated.

RIDER/EM: Cold.

GUARD: Welcome to Parchman.

RIDER/CJ: Body searched,

RIDER/EM: Again.

RIDER/DAYZ: Why?

GUARD: Because we can.

RIDER/EM: Hear the singing through the walls.

Same tune since slavery.

RIDER/CJ: My family be worrying.

GUARD: Too late now.

RIDER/EM: Freedom Riders all in prison.

We need more volunteers.

RIDER/DAYZ: To be stripped.

RIDER/CJ: Body searched.

RIDER/DAYZ: Humiliated.

RIDER/EM: Cold.

RIDER/CJ: To stand up.

POLICE/TY: Destination?

RIDER/DAYZ: Parchman.

POLICE: No sane person want to go to Parchman.

RIDER/CJ: Parchman.

POLICE: You crazy, right?

RIDER/EM: Parchman.

RIDER/DAYZ: I'm with them.

RIDER/EM: We're with them.

RIDER/CJ: Me too.

NEWSREADER/TY: If the authorities in Jackson are aiming to deter further Riders, it does not seem to be working. 50 more Freedom Riders were arrested in Jackson today on charges of breaching the peace.

Freedom RIDERS are having headshots, front and side, taken. They say their name as they face front.

Susan Hermann

Etta Simpson

William Mahoney

Rabbi Israel Dresner

Miller Greene

Joane Pleune

Alphonso Petway

Toma Greene

Lucretia Collins

Dr John Maguire

Gwendolyn Jenkins

Mary McCollum

Frederick Leonard

EM: And inside Parchman Prison still they refused to be cowed.

RIDER/DAYZ: *(Starts to sing.)*
    Buses are a coming, oh yes.
    Buses are a coming, oh yes

JAILER/TY: And none of that damn singing

    FRANCES and CJ join in singing.

RIDER/EM: *Better get you ready,*

JAILER: This a jailhouse, not a playhouse

RIDER/EM: *Better get you ready*

RIDER/DAYZ: What you going to do, send us to jail?

RIDER/EM: *Better get you ready, oh yes.*

JAILER: We hear one more peep out of you, we gonna take your mattress.

RIDERS: *(Singing.) You can take our mattress, oh yes*

Carry on singing underneath

JAILER: We'll take away your toothbrushes.

RIDERS: *You can take our toothbr… /*

RIDER/DAYZ: Hold on. How many of us in this cell?

RIDER/EM: 8

RIDER/DAYZ: In a cell designed for two? That's real close for bad breath.

RIDER/EM: *(Singing with mouth shut.) You can take our toothbrushes, oh yes*

They carry on humming the song underneath the news report.

NEWSREADER/TY: The eyes of the world are focused firmly on events unfolding here in Jackson Mississippi, where the number of Freedom Riders sent to the notorious Parchman prison now stands at 300. And still they keep on coming, more each day, from all across America. Men and women of all races and creeds are leaving their homes to get on buses, trains, and planes to merge with the students and overflow the jail cells of Jackson. Nothing is going to stop the Freedom Rides. Nothing is going to stop this movement. Dan Topolski, CBS News.

Cos they can't lock us all up.

Oh no.

I'm saying there ain't no building big enough to hide every citizen.

Ain't no country small enough the world can't see you,

See what you doing, see where you going. So give me a ticket, a ticket, a ticket,

Ticket to Jackson,

One way,

One way.

People in their houses in the suburbs or the cities,

Out in the boondocks, down among the pasture

Where you know it doesn't really,

Really,

Really, my friend,

Trouble us

What goes down out there in the world, somewhere else,

Next city,

Next state.

These people who ride through our community,

Take their lives in their hands for the sake of unity,

Of each for each other,

Mother, father, sister, brother,

Cousin, granma and aunt.

Because they can't,

No they can't,

They can't,

They can't lock us all up.

They are hearing through the wires of communication,

Through the wings of birds flying south on migration,

That the place to be,

To be seen,

To be heard,

To be hurt,

Is Jackson, Jackson, Jackson, Mississippi.
Front of the bus, yes sir, that's where I'm sitting.
Next train to,
Next plane to
Jackson, Jackson, Jackson, Mississippi.

PATTERSON/CJ: As Governor I knew the thing was over.
And then we began to lick our wounds.

EM: By the end of the summer of 61, with the eyes of the world
upon America and the Freedom Rides, Attorney General,
Robert Kennedy had no choice but to make sure the laws
desegregating interstate travel were actively enforced.

BOBBY K/CJ: I kid you not. Anyone found breaking these laws,
anywhere in the United States of America, will face the
consequences of their action and will be prosecuted with
the full weight of the law.

TY: Thanks to the Freedom Riders.

EM: And those who walked the road before them.

BRITISH ACTORS: SPOKEN WORD: ENSEMBLE
This is the thing.
Though the time seems long,
Your days don't have to be like this
For ever.
This is your business,
This living business,
This loving business,
This being alive.
This is the thing.
You have a choice,
A voice,
To use,
To lose.

One bead on the necklace leads to another.
Footprints on the road mean it's been walked before
By a sister, a brother,
Before
Your
Days began.
This is the thing.
They were expected to surrender.
They have not surrendered.
A little girl's kindness in a field of flame.
A teenager refusing to play the game,
And give up her seat on account of her race,
Know her place,
Take shame.
Instead, like Rosa Parks, she leave her name
To history and to those who came
And took action after.
They were expected to surrender.
They have not surrendered.
This is the thing.
This is your business,
This living business,
This loving business,
This being alive.
This is the thing.
You have a choice,
A voice,
To use,
To lose.
One bead on the necklace leads to another.
Footprints on the road mean it's been walked before
By a sister, a brother
Before
Your
Days began.

DAYZ puts her hand up to speak. The others look at her. She takes a deep breath, determined.

EM: What?

DAYZ: I want to say something.
There was a girl, called Dolores.

The others make way for her.

DOLORES/DAYZ: I got up one morning in summer and said to my folks, I won't be back today because I'm a Freedom Rider. It was like a wave or a wind that you didn't know where it was coming from or where it was going, but you knew you were supposed to be there. Nobody asked me. Nobody told me. It was like putting yeast in bread. It just rose up

VO: *Vox pop of British children's voices saying what they would like to change in their world.*